W9-DBQ-515

CHAMPIONS LEAGUE
LEGENDS

BY JONATHAN AVISE

SUPER SOCCER

SportsZone

An Imprint of Abdo Publishing
abdobooks.com

abdobooks.com

Published by Abdo Publishing, a division of ABDO, PO Box 398166, Minneapolis, Minnesota 55439. Copyright © 2019 by Abdo Consulting Group, Inc. International copyrights reserved in all countries. No part of this book may be reproduced in any form without written permission from the publisher. SportsZone™ is a trademark and logo of Abdo Publishing.

Printed in the United States of America, North Mankato, Minnesota
092018
012019

Cover Photos: Mike Egerton/PA Wire. URN:37482177/Press Association/AP Images, foreground; Shutterstock Images, ball
Interior Photos: Shutterstock Images, 1; Murad Sezer/AP Images, 4–5, 6; Phil Noble/AP Images, 8; Mirrorpix/Splash News/Newscom, 10–11; Real Madrid Exclusive/Getty Images, 12; PA Wire. URN:31507409/Press Association/AP Images, 14; Don Morley/Allsport/Hulton Archive/Getty Images, 16–17; Ricardo/AP Images, 19; Martin Meissner/AP Images, 20; Paul White/AP Images, 22–23; Sergey Ponomarev/AP Images, 25; Joan Valls/NurPhoto/Sipa USA/Newscom, 27; Angel Boluda/Action Plus/Getty Images, 28

Editor: Bradley Cole
Series Designer: Laura Polzin

Library of Congress Control Number: 2018949090

Publisher's Cataloging-in-Publication Data

Names: Avise, Jonathan, author.
Title: Champions League legends / by Jonathan Avise.
Description: Minneapolis, Minnesota : Abdo Publishing, 2019 | Series: Super soccer |
    Includes online resources and index.
Identifiers: ISBN 9781532117435 (lib. bdg.) | ISBN 9781641856256 (pbk) |
    ISBN 9781532170294 (ebook)
Subjects: LCSH: UEFA Champions League (Soccer tournament)--Juvenile literature. |
    World soccer stars--Juvenile literature. | European football--Juvenile literature. | Soccer
    players--Juvenile literature.
Classification: DDC 796.3346--dc23

★ TABLE OF ★ CONTENTS

CHAPTER 1

THE MIRACLE OF ISTANBUL

The 2005 Champions League Final in Istanbul, Turkey, was less than 60 seconds in, and Liverpool Football Club (FC) already found itself behind. The nightmarish start would only get worse.

By halftime, opponent AC Milan had added two more goals. All looked lost for Liverpool, trailing 3–0 with 45 minutes to play. The Italians were embarrassing the club from the northwest of England.

But Liverpool was not willing to give up that night. Captain Steven Gerrard started the comeback. Gerrard grew up near Liverpool as a supporter of the Reds. He joined the club's youth academy when he was nine years old and signed a professional

AC Milan immediately took the lead against Liverpool in the 2005 Champions League Final.

Liverpool kept itself in the game when midfielder Xabi Alonso made his second attempt past the goalkeeper.

contract at 17. Now he was leading his boyhood club as it fought to recover in its biggest match in years.

Liverpool's opening came in the 54th minute. Gerrard rose to meet a cross and headed the ball into the back of the net. Two minutes later it was Vladimir Smicer's turn. The Czech bombed a long-range shot that scooted past Milan's goalkeeper. Suddenly it was 3–2.

Now Liverpool had all the momentum. Soon Gerrard was steaming toward the goal like a locomotive when he was clipped from behind. The referee signaled a penalty kick. Milan keeper Dida saved Xabi Alonso's first attempt from the penalty spot. But midfielder Alonso followed his shot and punched home the rebound to tie the game 3–3.

"We thought it was all over," read the *Liverpool Echo* newspaper report on the game. "It wasn't."

Milan was stunned. In front of 40,000 fans from England, Liverpool had tied a match that had seemed all but over minutes before. In the span of six minutes, their night had gone from a nightmare to a dream.

Few clubs have had more success in the Champions League than Liverpool. The Reds had won the competition four times prior to 1992, when the tournament was known as simply the European Cup.

AC Milan is Champions League royalty too. The *Rossoneri*, Italian for "the red and blacks," were six-time champions. Only Real Madrid had won more. Milan was home to some of the most famous players in the world.

Liverpool players celebrate goalkeeper Jerzy Dudek's amazing save to win the 2005 Champions League final.

Now the two Champions League giants would go to extra time in Istanbul. Liverpool keeper Jerzy Dudek made two incredible saves from point-blank range to keep the game even.

And after a scoreless 30 minutes, the match moved into a shootout where he made two more huge saves.

The Reds had converted three of their four attempts, leaving Andriy Shevchenko as AC Milan's last hope. The star striker sent his penalty kick right down the middle. Dudek reached out a hand to stop it, and it was all over. Liverpool had done it.

Red and yellow confetti rained down on the field in Istanbul. Liverpool's thousands of fans in the stadium roared. Gerrard clutched the big handles of the European Cup and thrust it into the sky. The Miracle of Istanbul was complete.

ANOTHER ENGLISH COMEBACK

Liverpool isn't the only team to pull off a famous comeback to win the Champions League. Its old rival, Manchester United, pulled off the feat in May of 1999. With David Beckham, Roy Keane, Ryan Giggs, and Paul Scholes, United had one of the best teams in the world. Bayern Munich led 1–0 in stoppage time. Two Manchester United substitutes sprang to action and scored two shocking goals in three minutes. That took United from a devastating loss to a thrilling stoppage-time win.

CHAPTER 2

REAL MADRID GOES 5-FOR-5

In a tournament made up of Europe's best teams, one club stands out from the rest in the history of the Champions League. When people think of the European Cup, many think of only one team: Real Madrid.

The club is certainly one of Europe's most glamorous. Much of that reputation is built on a history of success in the world's biggest club tournament. And it all began at the very start of the European Cup. Real Madrid captured the first five cups from 1956 to 1960. Its success helped grow both the tournament's legend and its own.

Organized professional soccer had been played in countries across Europe since the late 1800s. But no formal continental club competition existed until the mid-1950s. It was created

Real Madrid led an aggressive attack against Manchester United's goalie Ray Wood, *top*, in the 1957 European Cup.

Alfredo Di Stéfano, *left*, led Real Madrid to the first five European Cup titles.

by the French sports newspaper *L'Equipe*. The paper aimed to crown a true club champion of Europe.

The tournament immediately set itself apart from the grind of domestic leagues. Its games matched the very best teams against one another. For the first five years of the tournament, the best of the very best was Real Madrid.

The team was led by hard-charging forward Alfredo Di Stéfano. Known as "the Blond Arrow," he was the heart and soul of the club. Di Stéfano led Madrid up and down the field. He defended aggressively. He controlled the midfield with expert passing and organization. He led lightning-quick counterattacks to catch the opposition off guard. He was a versatile player who excelled on every part of the pitch.

In the 1955–56 tournament, Madrid defeated three clubs in two-legged ties to reach the final in Paris. There they managed a narrow 4–3 victory over French club Stade de Reims to win the first-ever European Cup. The next season they defeated Manchester United on their way to a final at home in Madrid. Real Madrid again emerged with a victory, this time over ACF Fiorentina. A year later, the mighty Italian club AC Milan fell to Real Madrid in the final, 3–2 in extra time. In 1958–59 Real Madrid won an almost unthinkable fourth consecutive European Cup. They lifted the trophy after downing Reims again in the final.

Then came the bow on their five years of European dominance. The team was aging. Di Stéfano was slowing.

Real Madrid won the last Cup of its amazing five-year run at the 1960 final in Glasgow.

Madrid's La Liga rival, FC Barcelona, stood in the way of a fifth straight appearance in the finals.

In a tense two-legged semifinal, Madrid found its way past the club that had won the past two Spanish league championships. Now it was off to the final and a date with history. Madrid met Eintracht Frankfurt in Glasgow, Scotland.

Nearly 130,000 people packed the stadium to see Real Madrid make history.

"Man has five senses and five fingers on each hand," club chairman Santiago Bernabéu told the players before the game. "You have four European Cups." At the end of the night, they had five. It was a 7–3 demolition of the German side. Star forward Ferenc Puskás netted an incredible four goals. Di Stéfano added three of his own.

REPEAT WINNERS

No team has ever repeated Real Madrid's incredible feat of winning five straight European Cups. But other teams have been crowned repeat champions. Real Madrid won three straight from 2016 to 2018. AC Milan, Nottingham Forest for England, Liverpool, Bayern Munich, Ajax, Internazionale, and Benfica have all repeated wins at least once.

The win gave Madrid its fifth consecutive European Cup. It is a feat that has never been matched. The club won its 13th Champions League Cup in 2018. Madrid is still the most successful club in the history of the tournament. But nothing has matched the dazzling run of five straight European Cups.

CHAPTER 3

LITTLE MINNOWS WIN THE BIG CUP

The Champions League is the realm of soccer royalty. For most of its history, the Champions League and the silver European Cup have been the personal possession of Europe's biggest clubs. Giants such as Real Madrid, AC Milan, Barcelona, Liverpool, Juventus, and Manchester United have all laid claim to the cup.

But once in a while, the competition's little minnows beat the big fish to the top. Teams such as Celtic in 1967, Steaua Bucharest in 1986, and FC Porto in 2004 weren't expected to beat Europe's top clubs. But they all lifted the cup.

Clubs from Spain, Italy, and Portugal dominated the early years of what then was called the European Cup. When the 1966–67 tournament began, no team from England or Scotland

Bobby Lennox of Celtic FC helped lead a team that never quit attacking.

had ever reached a European Cup Final. Glasgow's Celtic FC would change that.

Celtic had qualified for its first European Cup in 1966 by winning the Scottish First Division. Nicknamed "the Bhoys," the club braved difficult games in Eastern Europe to make its way to Lisbon, Portugal, and the final against Internazionale of Milan. Known as Inter Milan, the Italians were heavily favored. With an impregnable defense, they had won the cup twice in three years.

But after falling behind early in the game, Celtic never stopped attacking. The Scottish squad punched two second-half goals in from close range to take the lead. Celtic would hold on and shock Inter and the soccer world. Celtic fans in their green and white rushed the field. It earned Celtic's 1967 team a new nickname: the Lisbon Lions.

Western European clubs from England, Spain, and Germany have had most of the success in the Champions League. With smaller budgets and fewer stars, Eastern European teams have had a hard time advancing in the Champions League and

Steaua Bucharest goalkeeper Helmuth Duckadam played a pivotal role in winning the 1986 European Cup for his team.

European Cup. Steaua Bucharest's victory in the 1986 final over powerful Barcelona wasn't just a surprise. It was unimaginable.

Barcelona had never won the European Cup before. But it had downed defending champion Juventus on the way to the final. All that stood in the way of Barcelona's first cup was a Romanian army team that was little known in the rest of Europe.

It was expected to be a cakewalk for the Spanish stars. Nearly 70,000 Barcelona fans had made the trip to the final in

Carlos Alberto scores the first goal of the final in a dominant performance for FC Porto.

the Spanish city of Seville. But Steaua's airtight defense kept Barcelona from scoring. And then, after a scoreless 120 minutes, Steaua's brick wall of a goalkeeper ruined the party for good.

Helmuth Duckadam stopped four Barcelona penalty kicks in the shootout. Two Steaua players converted their kicks, and one of the most shocking results in the history of the competition was complete. It would be almost 20 years before another significant upset shocked the Champions League.

In 2004 just seconds remained in the second leg of FC Porto's knockout stage match against powerful Manchester United. The underdogs looked set to exit the tournament.

Then the unthinkable happened. A free kick bounced off the Manchester goalkeeper. Porto's forward pounced and calmly kicked the ball into the back of the net.

The Portuguese team was through into the next round. It came at the expense of one of the most famous soccer clubs in the world. Porto's manager, José Mourinho, sprinted down the sideline to celebrate with his players.

Portugal's FC Porto had won the European Cup once before, in 1987. Now it was the Champions League, and smaller clubs found it harder to advance very far against the bigger teams. There was now a group stage to navigate before the knockout rounds began.

But that year, favorites such as Juventus, AC Milan, and Arsenal began to fall. Meanwhile, Porto and France's AS Monaco continued to win. It led to an unexpected final between the two clubs. Porto easily won 3–0 over AS Monaco to become one of the unlikeliest champions since the competition was renamed the Champions League in 1992. Soon after, Mourinho moved to Chelsea. But he left a Champions League title as his parting gift to Porto.

CHAPTER 4

CHAMPION OF CHAMPIONS

Under the stadium lights of Europe, Cristiano Ronaldo shines brightest. He struts, he poses, he glares. Most of all, the Portuguese mega-star scores in the biggest club competition in the world. The sight of Ronaldo tearing off his jersey after scoring a crucial goal has become a common Champions League sight. The high-scoring forward has netted more than 120 goals in Europe's most glamourous competition. That's a record-setting total that will be difficult to surpass.

Among those are goals that have clinched the cup for his club, Real Madrid. With Ronaldo leading the way, Madrid has gone on a historic run of success. The club, nicknamed *Los Blancos* for their white uniforms, captured consecutive Champions League titles in 2016, 2017, and 2018. That streak

Cristiano Ronaldo has scored more goals than any other player while playing for some of the biggest clubs in the Champions League.

followed the club's victory in 2014. Ronaldo also played a key role in Manchester United's 2008 triumph.

Ronaldo's professional debut came on Europe's biggest stage. His first appearance as a professional player came as a 17-year-old for Portuguese club Sporting Lisbon in August 2002. In an early-season Champions League game against Inter Milan, the hyped youngster came off the bench. He wowed the crowd with his dribbling but did little else. It was a quiet beginning for a player who would go on to make so much noise.

Three seasons later the young star found the net for the first time in Champions League play. By then, Ronaldo played for Manchester United. More than 100 Champions League goals followed for Ronaldo while playing for two of the world's biggest soccer clubs, United and Madrid.

Ronaldo delivered in the brightest spotlights. It took just 26 minutes for the powerful forward to rise to the occasion in a Champions League final. In the first half of the 2008 final in Moscow, he out jumped a Chelsea defender on a rainy pitch. He met a cross with his head. Ronaldo powered it past the rival goalkeeper, giving his side a 1–0 lead in the biggest game of his

Ronaldo showed off his athleticism while scoring the crucial goal against Chelsea.

career. It was Manchester's only regulation time goal in a win over its English Premier League rivals.

In 2014 Ronaldo sealed Real Madrid's 4–1 win in the Champions League Final over rival Atletico Madrid. He scored a league-record 17 goals in 10 Champions League matches.

In fact, Ronaldo led the Champions League in scoring six straight years, starting with the 2012–13 tournament. The incredible streak saw him outscore fellow stars such as Barcelona's Lionel Messi and Neymar. He truly is a star on the biggest stage in European soccer.

CHAPTER 5

BARCELONA SHOCKS PSG

FC Barcelona was finished. Paris Saint-Germain (PSG) had thumped the famous Spanish squad 4–0 in the first game of their 2017 Champions League knockout stage matchup. Teams advance in the knockout stage by outscoring their opponent over two games. A 4–0 deficit meant Barcelona would need to win Game 2 by at least that much to move on in the tournament. No team had ever climbed out of a hole that large in the Champions League.

Also, away goals serve as a tiebreaker. Barcelona didn't score in Paris, so if PSG scored even one goal in Barcelona, it would own that tiebreaker. Then Barcelona would have to win the second leg by at least five goals, or its Champions League journey would be over.

Lionel Messi, *right*, got things started for FC Barcelona by scoring an early goal in the match versus Paris Saint-Germain.

Neymar, *right*, helped Messi overcome incredible odds for FC Barcelona.

However, some teams just don't know how to give up. Barcelona would need an incredible performance to overcome the deficit. But it had the star-studded roster required to pull it off.

In front of 96,290 fans, the Spanish club scored twice in the game's first half. Barcelona was trying to put the pressure on PSG. Then Barcelona's biggest star, Lionel Messi, scored another five minutes after halftime to make it 3–0 on the day and 4–3 PSG in the aggregate. One more goal would force extra time and give Barcelona a chance.

But then disaster struck. PSG's Edinson Cavani scored. That made the combined score over two games 5–3. Barcelona now needed three more goals to complete the comeback.

Twenty-five minutes went by and still no more goals. Then another one of Barcelona's stars gave the team hope. As the clock hit 88 minutes, Neymar curled a magical free kick into the back of the net. Then the Brazilian converted a penalty kick in stoppage time. The combined score was now 5–5.

Because PSG had scored an away goal, it would move on if the game ended tied. Barcelona needed one more. With seconds remaining, Neymar played a pass over the nervous Paris defense. Sergi Roberto stretched out a leg. He caught the ball on the fly and sent it whizzing past the goalkeeper.

The famous Camp Nou stadium with its 100,000 Barcelona supporters exploded. Players ran in all directions, celebrating. The referee's whistle blew. Barcelona had done it. They had pulled off the biggest comeback in Champions League history.

"Any kid who was in the Camp Nou tonight will never forget this in their life," Barcelona's manager Luis Enrique told reporters after the match.

GLOSSARY

aggregate
The combined score of both games in a two-legged tie.

cross
A pass delivered from the side of the field toward the middle.

domestic league
A league made up of teams from the same country.

free kick
An unguarded kick awarded to a team after a foul.

group stage
The part of a tournament when teams are divided into smaller groups or pools; each team faces the others in the group, and those with the best records move on to the knockout stage.

knockout stage
A part of a competition in which one loss eliminates a team.

penalty kick
A play in which a shooter faces a goalkeeper alone; it is used to decide tie games or as a result of a foul.

stoppage time
Also known as added time, a number of minutes tacked onto the end of a half for stoppages that occurred during play from injuries, free kicks, and goals.

two-legged tie
A competition that matches two teams playing one game at each team's home stadium; the team with the most goals across the two games is the winner.

youth academy
A program run by a club to train young players and help them improve their skills.

MORE INFORMATION

BOOKS

Kortemeier, Todd. *Total Soccer*. Minneapolis, MN: Abdo Publishing, 2017.

Marquardt, Meg. *STEM in Soccer*. Minneapolis, MN: Abdo Publishing, 2018.

McDougall, Chrös. *The Best Soccer Players of All Time*. Minneapolis, MN: Abdo Publishing, 2015.

ONLINE RESOURCES

Booklinks
NONFICTION NETWORK
FREE! ONLINE NONFICTION RESOURCES

To learn more about the Champions League, visit **abdobooklinks.com**. These links are routinely monitored and updated to provide the most current information available.

INDEX

ABOUT THE AUTHOR

Jonathan Avise is a reporter, writer, and digital media editor from Minneapolis, Minnesota. An avid soccer fan, he is a die-hard supporter of North London's Tottenham Hotspur.

5